Learning About...

Evangelism

Mike Hencher

Christian Focus

ISBN 1-85792-738-9

© Copyright Mike Hencher 2002

Published in 2002
by
Christian Focus Publications, Ltd.
Geanies House, Fearn, Tain,
Ross-shire, IV20 1TW, Great Britain.

www.christianfocus.com

Cover Design by Alister MacInnes

Printed and bound by
Cox & Wyman, Cardiff Road, Reading

Contents

Mike Hencher has been involved in fulltime evangelism for 30 years. He began by working with the Movement for World Evangelisation and Don Summer's Evangelistic Association. He has worked with Trans World Radio and is a founder member of the Christian Television Association. He has recently completed an degree in Biblical Studies at the University of Gloustershire. Check out his website at www.themissingpeace.org

1

FRIENDSHIP EVANGELISM

Three steps to becoming a witness for Christ.

Having gained knowledge of our Lord Jesus Christ, how can it be shared with those who don't know Him? 'Friendship Evangelism' describes exactly the ordinary, day-by-day, sharing with others of the good news of Christ.

A few years ago I was invited to attend the first training course conducted by Search Ministries. I travelled to New England for a Bible Conference, and then down to Baltimore to the offices of this US-based, transdenominational, ministry. Some of the things I had the privilege of being taught, I'd like to pass on to you, weaving in with them some of my own experience and insights that will, I hope, encourage you in your witness.

If, this year, you were to reach one non-

Christian with the Gospel and he or she became a believer, year two would begin with the two of you reaching out. If, that year, you both win one each, there will be four of you. By the year 5 you multiply to 32. Year 10, and the number increases to 1,024; after 20 years, 1,048,576; and by year 33, over 8,500,000,000, the probable size of the world's population in the early 21st century!

It's a matter of 'each one reaching one' for Christ each year, and discipling that person to be ready 'to teach others also'. It's only maths, unfortunately, because not everyone will accept Christ. The real question, as far as we are concerned, is whether we will share the Gospel.

If I said to you, write down on your prayer list the names of five friends whom you are seeking to influence for Christ, would you be able to do that?

One of the reasons evangelistic methods of all kinds fail is simply because some Christians don't have any non-Christian friends at all! We have taken note of Paul's use of a quotation from Isaiah 52, when he writes in 2 Corinthians 6:17, 'Therefore come out from them' (referring to idol worshippers) '...and be separate'. Paul was giving a command from the Lord to Christians of all ages. Certainly we must not engage in anything sinful, but has our separateness actually become isolation?

The tension comes about because we are called to come out and be separate and, *at the same time*, our Master sends us into the world. What tends to happen in this tension is that some Christians allow the pendulum between the two, to swing hard over to the isolationist side so that they have no contact with non-Christians apart from what is absolutely unavoidable. The other extreme is to be totally immersed in the world. Those on the isolationist end of the spectrum have no meaningful contact with non-believers with whom to share the Gospel. The worldly Christian has the contacts all right, but he or she is so similar to the non-Christian that the unbeliever doesn't see any difference in lifestyle, and consequently doesn't see their need of Christ. Like most things in the Christian life, we have two extremes to avoid, and a balanced pathway in the centre to seek out and follow. So how do we go about doing that?

I. Find out exactly what Scripture says about our association with those who have not yet trusted Christ.

Everyone we meet, however good, bad or indifferent, should have the chance to hear the Gospel and see it lived out in front of them. Perhaps then the Spirit of God will stir up that person to repentance and faith. It's not our job to work out who should hear the Gospel and who should not, and we must remember that God the Holy Spirit deals differently with every one of us, to meet our individual needs at just the right time. So we must not say, 'Oh, he will not be interested in Christ' or, 'She is just so bad she would never want Christ to save her'; nor should we say that everybody has got to be converted in the same way.

The same God who made all our fingerprints differently, and who didn't even make two snowflakes alike, works in each person's life differently, in their unique circumstances, in His own time.

2 Corinthians 6:17 must also be seen in its context. Certainly a Christian should 'not be yoked together with unbelievers'. No Christian should marry an unbeliever hoping to change him or her afterwards. Occasionally God, in His grace, does that in *spite* of our wilful breaking of His command. This verse can also be applied to business partnerships. Being bound in a business with an unbeliever is most likely going to lead to the downfall of the believer. As in the marriage of darkness and light, they just don't mix.

But remember, we are speaking of separation, not isolation. Those who won't even eat a meal with their non-believing children are totally swinging to the extreme. At best they will not be the salt and light in the world that they should be; at worst they may cause many to say, 'If that's Christians for you, you can keep them!' God wants us *insulated*, not *isolated*. When we put on the 'full armour of God' of Ephesians 6, we are able to take our stand against the Devil's schemes; but we should never become so isolated from the world that we have no acquaintances to whom we can go with the Gospel.

2. Follow the model that Christ gave us.

Our Lord was totally without sin the whole of His life apart from the time when 'He Himself bore our sins in His body on the tree....' But He was accused of being a drunkard and a friend of tax collectors and sinners (Matthew 11:19). According to one count, the Gospels record 132 contacts that Jesus had with people. Six were in the Temple, four in the synagogues, and 122 out where the people were, in the mainstream of life! Christ *had* personal contact with sinners, yet He maintained a lifestyle of purity. The old cliché is true; He hated sin but He loved sinners.

3. Pursue personal spiritual maturity.

We will make no impact on our non-Christian friends without contact with them, but contact can be risky! The best way to make sure we don't fall into sin is to have a healthy walk with Christ so that we see this present evil, seductive, fascinating, world for what it *really* is. It is Satan's system for stealing the worship that God should receive. He tosses out idols for us to pick up and, by so doing, slip into sin. If we keep close to Christ He will give us His strength and effectiveness *in* the world while remaining not *of* the world. Christ must be our model—not anyone else!

Christ is our Great High Priest, who built a bridge between God and man. The Latin word for priest (*pontifex*) literally means 'bridge-builder'. We, as believer-priests, are also to be building bridges, as Christ did. He touched the untouchable lepers; He spoke to the prostitute and scandalised the religious community by mixing with the "riffraff".

John Stott in *Our Guilty Silence* said, 'We are to go as He went, to *penetrate* human society, to *mix* with unbelievers and to *fraternise* with sinners. Doesn't one of the Church's greatest failures lie here? We have disengaged too much. We have become *aloof* instead of *alongside*.'

'The more a Christian is like Jesus Christ, really like Jesus Christ', said Joe Aldrich in his terrific book *Life-Style Evangelism,* 'the more effective he is in evangelism....' Christ was characterised by a holy worldliness. This is the model for the believer. But it's risky. It's 'out with the wolves'; it's dangerous. When sheep are 'out with the wolves' they must obey and trust the shepherd; but when they hang around the barn [the church], who needs the shepherd?

If you decide to seek to win souls for Christ, there will be risk, criticism, heartache...but joy too as, together with the angels, you rejoice 'over one sinner who repents' (Luke 15:10).

Are you separated or isolated? Will you begin to reach out so that, as Paul put it, '...by all possible means I might save some' (1 Corinthians 9:22). That same verse in Kenneth Taylor's *Living Bible,* is paraphrased like this:

'...Yes, whatever a person is like, I try to find common ground with him so that he will let me tell him about Christ and let Christ save him'. We have to make the effort to meet our friends on common ground; we must be able to tell them what Christ has done for us; and then, perhaps this year, this month, this very day, Christ will save them.

Think of the people Christ has brought close to you. Begin to pray for them. Seek out opportunities to be with them...over coffee...in the garden...doing the decorating...and in time the Gospel can be shared.

'He who wins souls is wise' Proverbs 11:30

Must one be an expert?

One does not have to have the gift of an evangelist to share Christ effectively with others! Obviously, those in your church or assembly who have been given the gift of evangelism, are going to be more able than those of us who have other gifts of the Spirit. One of the most common difficulties that arises in our fellowships when we plan to reach out to the non-believer in Christ, is what I'll call 'expertitus'.

Many churches used to call an evangelist into their area once every three to five years. I've been involved in many of these with small local churches, on a city-wide basis, and nationally. It sometimes appears that we believe that by calling in Brother So-and-so, souls will be saved as a matter of course, because he is an expert! For many of us, evangelism is little more than us lining up 'fish' for the expert 'fisherman' to net for us. If we do go out into the community, we tend to go out on evangelistic safaris and 'ambush' the poor unsuspecting inhabitants. We use gimmicks like questionnaires or Gospel tracts to get into conversation. Most of us find this embarrassing and feel that we are intruding. This is mainly because we are!

The really successful churches spend many years building up a relationship with those living near the church, and wait for a natural opportunity to share Christ. They have realized that evangelism is a process, not a product; it's not instant, like so many of today's packaged goods. It's a process...very often a long process, of friendship leading to the opportunity to explain the good news of the Gospel.

Do you remember the verse from the Living Bible? '...Whatever a person is like, I try to find common ground with him so that he will let me tell him about Christ and let Christ save him' (1 Corinthians 9:22). We have to build bridges to our friends and neighbours if we really want to be a help to them. We don't have to be experts, knowing most of the answers contained in the Bible. People *do* want *some* answers, but first of all they want to know if we are really interested in *them*. Floyd McClung said it well , 'People don't care how much we know until they know how much we care'. For some years Floyd and his family placed themselves in the 'red light district' of Amsterdam: he knows what he's talking about! In a day when most Christians are moving out of the inner-city areas, he and his family chose to be in the thick of things. Not many of us can take that sort of pressure. But right where we are now, there are people with needs, and the answer to their deepest need is Jesus. How are they going to hear the good news?

Are we going to leave it to 'Songs of Praise', 'Sunday Half Hour', or perhaps the expert evangelists who use satellite television? The Lord wants us all to be involved.

Just think of the joy of leading a friend, neighbour, or relative to Christ! Yes, you, by yourself, under the leading and power of the Holy Spirit! You might even find that you have the gift of the evangelist and didn't know it. It's been suggested that over 10 per cent of Christians in our churches have such a gift. That doesn't mean that in an assembly of 100 believers there are 10 potential 'Billy Grahams'. Perhaps none of the 10 will ever be so-called 'full-time' evangelists. They will be the ones who can talk to neighbours over the garden fence. They will have taken the trouble to think about how to communicate with non-Christians and won't come out with meaningless jargon that the contact cannot comprehend. Perhaps you have the gift of inviting folks to come to church, and they come! When your friends are in need, they turn to you! You may not be an expert – whatever that means – but God has gifted you to help others to come closer to Christ. Then do as Paul wrote to Timothy, 'Fan into flame the gift of God, which is in you....' (2 Timothy 1:6) 'Do the work of an evangelist!' (2 Timothy 4:5)

A group from my church had shared the

Gospel with Val, and I was privileged to be present when she put her trust in the Lord. Soon afterwards she wrote her faith-story entitled, 'I Lived for Dances'. She typed out her story and it appeared in our church magazine; and then she made many copies. She took the sheets round the village, putting one in each home.

I Lived for Dances

Until about a year ago, yes, I lived for dances. Immediately one was over I would be looking at the calendar to see when the next was due, thinking about which dress I would wear, how I would have my hair done, etc. Always it was the same, a real gay time on the night, but the next day I was left feeling flat and wondering just what was it all about.

I was a comparatively happy person. I had a good marriage, two 'normal', healthy children, and a nice home and garden. In spite of this I often found myself wondering about life and what the meaning of it all was, but I was never aware that I had a need. Not, however, until Beryl invited me to a coffee evening at the nurses house in Huntley. I thought I had better show my face as both my children attended the Huntley Adventure Hour; and I was also curious to see what 'these people' who gave their time voluntarily were like. I now know it was all part of the Lord's plan for my salvation.

I felt like a fish out of water that night. Everyone there worshipped at one church or another, if only occasionally, whereas I only went to the end-of-term services out of duty to my children. I had never come up against people like Theo Cracknell and Mike Hencher before. I continued to go to these coffee-evenings and mornings, firstly just to enjoy the coffee and intriguing chat; but one cannot enter into conversation about the Lord and remain on the fence. There comes a time when one has to either accept Him or reject Him. Deep down everyone, whether they admit it or not, has a need. Many people try to fill this gap in their lives with material things, only to find that it still remains, very often, a bigger gap than before. I thank the Lord that I accepted Him.

This means that you believe that everything the Bible says about Jesus is true. That He came to earth as man and died on the cross for you, taking all your sins with Him. You realise this and acknowledge the fact that you cannot save yourself. Ephesians 2:8,9: 'For it is by His grace that you are saved through trusting Him and not by your own doing. It is God's gift and not a reward for work done.' You simply ask Him to come into your life and take over, telling Him that you are sorry for your sins. Romans 10:9,10 'if you confess that Jesus is Lord, believe that God raised Him from death, you will be saved. It is by faith that we are put right with God; it is by confession that we are saved'.

A year has almost passed since this. My life has changed and I have experienced a feeling of peace and contentment that I would never have believed possible. The Bible I once thought of as a dry old book has come to life as, day by day, I read God's Word. The born-again Christian still has problems like any other human being; but gradually I have learnt to take them to God in prayer, knowing that He always answers. He thus helps to solve all problems and worries.

As this year commenced I realized

for the first time in my life that I could look forward to a new year with confidence, knowing that, whatever may happen, the Lord is with me to guide and strengthen. I realize now that what I thought was coping, was merely muddling through.

My God is wonderful, and He can be your God too if you put your trust in Him. I no longer live for dances. I live for the Lord.'

I'd like you to notice some points that stand out in that testimony:

1) Even though this lady seemed to have everything, she often felt flat, 'wondering just what (life) was all about'. Your friends and neighbours do too... Will you tell them about your Saviour?

2) Beryl, who is not a public speaker, *privately* asked her to come to the home of two Christian nurses (three involved already). Other Christians had been running a children's meeting in the village. Theo, a church leader, had organised a great deal, and Mike Hencher (the so-called professional evangelist) came in to do his small part for the Lord.

3) Keep in the forefront of your mind how non-Christians feel when first they get involved with us. 'I felt like a fish out of water that night', this new Christian remembered a year later!

Here is a very practical suggestion. Take a couple of pieces of paper and write out the main points of *your* faith-story (i.e., how Christ drew you to Himself and what happened as a result). Write it as if you were telling it to the person that you would love to see trust Christ. Then read it out loud and time yourself. If you have used a lot of paper you will be too long. You may have to rewrite your story a few times before you reduce it to under two minutes. When you have done this you will be far more able to share your faith in clear and brief way.

Now let's summarise all of these thoughts: Experts play their part but, without other Christians praying and participating, nothing very much happens. You may not be an 'expert', but you may be an evangelist. Even if you are neither, if you know the Lord you can tell a friend how you trusted Christ. Don't let's forget the feelings of those we try to win for Christ. Let's do it sensitively and wisely to the glory of God.

2

Fear Factors

In chapter one we dealt with Isolation and Separation: the tension in which we all live, trying to keep ourselves from sin, but not avoiding non-Christians altogether. Bill Glass has described the attitude we should have like this, 'A Christian is not one who withdraws, but one who infiltrates.' Our Lord in His High Priestly prayer in John 17 said, 'My prayer is not that You take them out of the world but that You protect them from the evil one.' When you're sailing, the boat is in the water, but you don't want the water in the boat! Ralph L. Williams has said, 'We do not stand in the world bearing witness to Christ; we stand in Christ bearing witness to the world.'

Then we saw that the expert evangelist has his or her place, but that doesn't mean we leave it all to them. Satan likes to side-track us by making us think that we are dependent on the experts, and this keeps us from sharing Christ with our friends. Elsie Yale's familiar hymn says it all:

There's a work for Jesus,
    precious souls to bring,
Tell them of His mercies,
    tell them of your king,
Faint not, grow not weary,
    He will strength renew;
There's a work for Jesus,
    none but *you* can do.

In this chapter we will look at ways of helping us to face one of biggest stumbling-blocks to evangelism: FEAR!

This fear comes in many different forms to foul up our attempts at winning our friends for Christ. Some of the fear is real; and some is based on things that we believe to be true, but which are in fact lies.

Let's look at some of the factors that really do exist, which we must face.

I. People Blindness

There are an ever-increasing number of people with whom we come in contact day by day because of the way we now live. Cars and trains, telephones and aeroplanes, force us to relate to many more people today than years ago. There are so many relationships possible, that we find contact with our nearest and dearest difficult.

People are shown to us on TV in vast numbers all around the world. We can't cope with Asia's teeming millions; the numbers are too vast and, after a while, we develop 'people blindness': we don't see the need for missionaries abroad and at home, because the task is so great!

2. Busyness

The pace of life is such that we fear the demands on our time. We daren't offer to spend time with our non-Christian friends because we are so busy in our work and so wrapped up in maintaining the meetings at our church, perhaps because of declining numbers. One of the things I love about the Gospel record of the life of our Lord Jesus is the fact that He always had time to speak to people. Fear of spending too long with His disciples, or a needy person like the woman of Samaria, never entered His mind. Fear of spending time in prayer, even whole nights, had no place in our Lord's thinking. Yet He always did those things that pleased the Father and could say at the end of His life, 'I have brought You glory on earth by completing the work You gave me to do' (John 17:4). The Lord restricted Himself to doing only what God wanted Him to do, and completing it. He didn't heal or convert everyone in Israel. He left His disciples to continue His work after His ascension.

Have you found yourself becoming a Christian workaholic? There's a need in the Sunday School , so you volunteer. The youth club leader has moved, so you dive in. Publicity is desperately required yesterday, so you burn the midnight oil. It's one of the subtlest schemes of the enemy to prevent us worshipping Christ. We just haven't time to read our Bibles or pray. Our spouse suffers. We put the kids off with a, 'not now, I'm too busy!' Our work for God has become an idol!

God's will for our lives is to look after our families and only do the work He wants us to do, not the workloads of others too! So we get fearful over the size of the task. We find the pace of life fast and complicated enough without risking time-consuming relationships with our unsaved friends to introduce them to the Lord.

3. Evangelistic techniques that make us uncomfortable

We have all tried (or been pushed into) methods of evangelism that failed in the past and cause fear for the present. Confronting non-Christians on their doorstep armed with a leaflet or invitation, strikes fear into most of us. We need to find a method of evangelism with which we are comfortable and have the spiritual gifts to accomplish. From my experience, being friends with folk is bound to have a greater effect than bombarding all of our area with Gospel booklets.

The book of Acts teaches us to begin at our Jerusalem, where we live; then to reach out to the stranger in the 'Samarias' around us; and finally 'to the ends of the earth' (Acts 1:8). I heard of an estate agency that divided their city into 'farms' of 500 families each. An agent was responsible to make contact with each home in his 'farm' once a month by phone, letter, or personal visit. It took at least six contacts for a homeowner to remember the agent; but if the representative maintained that pattern for eighteen months, he would receive eighty per cent of the business in his area! If an estate agent can show interest from merely a financial motive, surely we in the same way can show interest in our neighbours out of eternal motives.

How about writing down the names of a 'five-family farm' with whom we can become well acquainted? Even that may cause fear. Prayerfully consider whom the Lord would have us focus upon, and begin to pray for them, you only have to begin with one family or person. Picture the Holy Spirit of God hovering over your neighbourhood. As you walk by the houses, ask the Lord who is ready to respond. Extend your social relationships: baby-sit; help with car repairs; go fishing; do a favour; have coffee or a barbecue together.

Reaching out in friendship is not confrontational and is most likely to succeed. One-to-one evangelism is the basis of all evangelistic outreach. Whom do you have close to you? Will you pray for them by name and by friendship influence them for Christ?

3

Cultivation

Sometime ago, 558 people, half the population of a village in India, embraced another faith, not Christianity. When asked why, they said that Christian concern for people ended with their conversion, while the other faith looked after them following their conversion too. We use the term 'soul-winning' a great deal; but perhaps the concept of 'soul-caring' is an area we can develop.

Our Lord's encounter with the rich young ruler illustrates the difference between soul-winning and soul-caring. We can always care, but we can't always win. Mark 10:21 records that 'Jesus looked at him and loved him'. And yet the young man, at least at that time, rejected Jesus' offer of eternal life and 'went away sad' – Jesus cared, but in this instance didn't 'win'. I wonder if this young man changed his mind later on.

Stan Mooneyham, former President of World Vision, offers this explanation on the subject: 'It seems to me that 'winning' is a self-centred concept. Caring is an other-directed concept. To win you have to come in ahead of someone else. You are in a competition. When the focus is on being a winner, the soul tends to become secondary, almost an afterthought'. He concludes, 'Winning just may not be the best word. When we bring good news to someone in despair, we don't say we 'win' the despairing one. If there is any 'winner' in soul-winning, it is surely the one who hears and acts upon the good news, not the one who transmits it'.

In these next few studies we will hang our thoughts on a very important word in evangelism: cultivation. How can we successfully cultivate the soil of our friends' soul?

I. Test the soil

Is it heavy or soft, acid or alkaline? What other properties does it have?

In evangelism we must test the soil of the lives with whom we are seeking to share Christ, so that we know the best way to promote growth in Christ. If the soul-soil is able to receive the message we wish to plant, that's fine. If not, we will have to do some work at this level before we can sow the Gospel seed. Muck-spreading seems to be a universal method of promoting growth! It's not a very glamorous job and the smell takes a bit of getting used to! But evangelism isn't a glamour job either. Farmers expect to work hard and long. If we want to see our friends come to Christ, we will have to be prepared to get involved in tough tasks where the smell of the world will, sometimes literally, cling to our clothes. To reach our friends we have to care enough to put ourselves out. The 'fertiliser of friendship' must be applied liberally to prepare for growth.

2. Prepare for planting

The ploughing that sin produces in a life very often makes it desperate for God. Life's circumstances, the pain of disease and death, lay open lives to allow the penetration of the Gospel message.

A Special Police Constable I know began to think of Christ when he saw a Bible on the dashboard of a crumpled sports car from which the driver, miraculously, had walked unhurt. He thought if God could get His people out of that sort of crash, He must be a powerful, caring God. The Lord was at work in our lives long before we trusted in Christ.

3. Sow the seed

As we cultivate the soil, by doing our part in this process of evangelism, we can all rejoice together.

'I tell you,' said Jesus in John 4:35, 'open your eyes and look at the fields! They are ripe for harvest. Even now the reaper draws his wages, even now he harvests the crop for eternal life, so that the sower and the reaper may be glad together. Thus the saying "One sows and another reaps" is true. I sent you to reap what you have not worked for. Others have done the hard work, and you have reaped the benefits of their labour.'

4. Care for the plants

Some housebound folk say to me, 'I can't do anything for the Lord; all I can do is pray!' Prayer is work, very hard work. Prayer is evangelism. Sometimes there's nothing humanly we can do except pray. So if you have that job for the Lord in the process of evangelism, then prayer-water those plants in whom the good news is sown until growth produces a bumper harvest.

5. Reap the harvest

Those who reap the harvest don't have to be experts. Perhaps not many of us would wish to speak to thousands, but to lead our friends and neighbours to Christ, as part of a long process in which we and others have been involved, is very natural. As Paul told the church at Corinth, '...the

Lord has assigned to each his task. I planted the seed, Apollos watered it, but God made it grow. So neither he who plants nor he who waters is anything, but only God, who makes things grow' (1 Corinthians 3:6).

6. Bring the grain into the barn

After the reaping, the grain has to be brought into the barn: the church. If you have been involved in any missions, you will know the problem of linking up converts with churches in a satisfactory way. Nurture groups are a means of looking after converts, in homes usually, where the basic steps in living the Christian life are shared and practised. But when they are invited into the 'barn', the church, some find a frosty atmosphere or an over-cuddly contact, and it is too much for them. They never make it to the last stage of evangelism, which is to:

7. Bake the bread

Those we lead to the Lord are babes in Christ who need to be brought to maturity. They need help; some of the stench of the old life will still be hanging around. We have to minister to them, often with no thanks from them, but it will be worth it when they, in turn, win their friends to Christ, and when we see them grow in maturity in their faith.

4

Communicate

If we take the first letters of the word CULTIVATE, it helps us to remember what we are trying to do in evangelism.

Communicate
Understand the world
Listen with love
Talk and walk
Invest in common ground
Value the person
Answer their questions
Tell the truth
Expect God's harvest

Communicate with God

When was the last time you heard a sermon on prayer for the lost? It's amazing how little time we spend in prayer for our friends and neighbours, to help them to trust Christ. How do I know? It's a weakness in my life too.

Sometimes my trust seems to be in the techniques of men, instead of talking to God.

I have many modern books about evangelism in my study and most of them say very little about communicating with God. One manual, over 300 pages thick, has just five pages on prayer! We believe that prayer is somehow not as important as other things we do. John Blanchard has written, 'Prayer is not the least we can do, it is the most'. You can evangelise directly by praying for your friends, and to back up others at home and abroad who are preaching Christ crucified. Prayer knows no bounds or barriers.

If the up-to-date books on evangelism seem a bit light on the matter of prayer, some of the older ones major on God's power and our prayers to plead for His action on behalf of lost souls. Oswald J. Smith finishes his book, *The Passion for Souls*, by saying, 'He who would preach powerfully must pray effectively'. Billy Graham has said, 'If I had my time over again, I would preach less and pray more'. Here is God's secret for effective evangelism. Not our efforts, skill and talents, but fervent prayer. We can ALL do that!

We seem to have forgotten God's principles for effective evangelism. We have the high-tech approach today, with every advantage, humanly speaking; but we forget too often to communicate with God about our friends before we try to evangelise them. There is a Hebrew proverb which says, 'He who prays for his neighbour will be heard for himself'. Perhaps the blockage in the flow of God's blessing in our lives is partly due to our lack of concern for the lost souls that surround us, who are slipping into Hell. In one city-wide crusade I was involved in, up in the Midlands, I was given the task of leading the prayer meeting. It was supposed to be the big push as far as prayer was concerned for the whole area. Just one other person turned up, an elderly lady in a wheelchair! We had a great time of prayer together, but where was everyone else?

To anchor our study, let's look at Ephesians 6:18-20. As we go through these verses let's ask ourselves *how* we should communicate with God, *for* whom should we pray, and *what* should we say. Someone has wisely said, 'Talk to God about people before you talk to people about God'.

'*And pray in the Spirit...*' Charles Finney once wrote, 'Commonly those who pray long in a meeting do so, not because they have the spirit of prayer, but because they have not. Some men will spin out a long prayer in telling God who and what He is as if He were in doubt. Or they pray out a whole system of divinity. Some preach; others exhort the people till everybody wishes they would stop, and God does too. They should keep to the point, and pray for what the Spirit of God is doing and not follow the imaginations of their own hearts and pray vaguely all over the universe!'

'...*on all occasions with all kinds of prayers and requests*'. We pray specifically for those families and friends God has brought to our minds. They may have health needs, financial problems, or tensions in their marriages. Their children may be causing heartache or the husband may have lost his job and be unable to find work. When we contact our friends and care for their needs, there's no shortage of prayer topics.

'...*be alert*'. The Kingdom of God needs praying Christians. Our friends need our prayers. We need our prayers. Leonard Ravenhill is quoted as saying, 'The self-sufficient do not pray; the self-satisfied will not pray; the self-righteous cannot pray. No man is greater than his prayer life'. Do you find the long haul of prayer difficult? We start praying for people and as the weeks go by we lose heart or concentration, and we forget them. Kenneth Wilson has written:

There's something exquisitely luxurious about room service in a hotel. All you have to do is pick up a phone and somebody is ready and waiting to bring you breakfast, lunch, dinner, chocolate milkshake, whatever your heart desires and your stomach will tolerate. Or by another languid motion of the wrist, you can telephone for someone who will get a soiled shirt quickly transformed into a clean one or a rumpled suit into a pressed one. That's the concept that some of us have of prayer. We have created God in the image of a divine bellhop. Prayer, for us, is the ultimate in room service, wrought by direct dialling. Furthermore, no tipping, and everything charged to that great credit card in the sky. Now prayer is many things, but I'm pretty sure this is not one of the things it is.

For whom should we pray? '*...for all the saints*' and then Paul says, 'Pray also *for me*'. This wasn't a selfish desire. He wanted God's power to open his mouth. If one of your fears is speaking out for the Lord, perhaps someone close to you will pray for strength for you in this area. Paul asks for prayer that he might share the secrets of the Gospel 'fearlessly'. If Paul was scared, why are we surprised if fear sweeps over us! Communicating with God is the answer.

Communicating with God about our unsaved friends will open the way for us to get to know them better and be able to tell them what Christ has done for us and would love to do for them. Pray for reasonable things...that you might get in conversation with them; that they will accept a book or a tape from you, perhaps attend a special service, or come into your home for a chat. As

God answers these small requests, we can go on to pray for an opportunity to share the Gospel with our friends and invite them to receive Christ.

5

Understand the World

The Greek word '*kosmos*', meaning the ordered world, is used sometimes for what we would call the universe, i.e., the stars and planets of the solar system. But because mankind is the most important part of the universe, the word 'kosmos' is more often used in the limited sense of the human beings living on planet earth. Because sin has entered the human race, John in particular used the word 'world' in the sense of the disfigured world. When he talks about 'this world', he means the world as it is now, not as God intended it to be. So when we talk about 'the world', we are really speaking about the things, attitudes, and people who, mostly unknowingly, follow 'the prince of this world', as John calls the enemy (John 12:31).

In his first letter, chapter 2 verses 14 and following, John writes, '...the Word of God lives in you' (speaking, of course, to Christians), 'and you have overcome the evil one'. Then he gives us a strong warning that applies to the whole of the Christian life, and especially in the area of evangelism.

If we get absorbed by the world, we will lose all power in evangelism. John commands:

'Do not love the world or anything in the world. If anyone loves the world, the love of the Father is not in him. For everything in the world – the cravings of sinful man, the lust of his eyes and the boasting of what he has and does – comes not from the Father but from the world'.

The two prominent features of the world are **pride** and **covetousness**. Pride, because those who have not surrendered to the Lord of creation are, in fact, fighting against Him. The coveting of things is so much part of our society today that everyone knows what is motivating most of us...money! Our friends have the worldview of the age. When we reach out to them, we must understand how they feel and what is in their minds.

If we look at 2 Corinthians 4:3-4, God tells us what is happening to our friends. We need to be reminded, because we Christians so often forget that there was a time, maybe in the distant past or even quite recently, that we did not know Christ and we *were* as these verses describe: blind!

'And even if our Gospel is veiled, it is veiled to those who are perishing. The god of this age has blinded the minds of unbelievers, so that they cannot see the light of the Gospel of the glory of Christ, who is the image of God'

We mentioned in our last chapter that prayer is not stressed in books on evangelism. Understanding the unsaved is also only referred to rarely. If we got our prayer life right and understood our friends' feelings in their lost condition, we would be well on the way to being of real spiritual help to them. So, once again we will look at what God says in His Word.

The first word for us to check out is **veiled**. Paul says the good news of the Gospel is 'veiled to those who are perishing'.

He is referring back to chapter 3:13. The veil there is the one Moses put 'over his face to keep Israelites from gazing at it while the radiance was fading away'. Moses' face was shining after speaking with God and seeing His glory pass by. Speaking of the believers, 3:18 says, '...we, who with unveiled faces all reflect the Lord's glory, are being transformed into His likeness with ever-increasing glory, which comes from the Lord, who is the Spirit'. And the thought is expanded in verse 14, '...their minds were made dull, for to this day the same veil remains when the old covenant is read'.

Our friends of whatever faith have to have this veil removed if they are ever going to see the beauties of Jesus. Chapter 3, verse 16, explains what has happened to us and what we should pray about for our friends, 'But whenever anyone turns to the Lord, the veil is taken away'. The veil over people's minds is there through unbelief. But the enemy is responsible for encouraging unbelief in the human heart. What he began with Adam and Eve, has swept like a forest fire through the lives of everyone since. Paul accuses the 'god of this age,' Satan, for this blindness.

The one who is doing the damage to your friends is 'the prince of this world', as he is also called. His other names, 'the prince of darkness' and 'the ruler of the darkness of this world', describe his heinous crime against humanity. The darkness in our friends' understanding, promotes their prejudices and expands the error they have in their minds. They are totally **blinded**. We must always remember that. Perhaps they will say things and do things that seem to us incredibly stupid and wrong, but they can't help it. We must allow them to express themselves and thrash around in their darkness until the light dawns.

Now that you have five names or families on your list, you can actively pray against the blindness of your contacts, releasing them from the darkness so that they can 'see' what we are sharing. Our hearts always go out to someone physically blind, but we often don't respond to their needs in a knowledgeable way due to lack of understanding. Let us make sure, in this eternal blindness from which our friends are suffering, that we understand what they think and feel; and let's be aware that apart from the work of the Holy Spirit, they just cannot see!

The other thing that this verse teaches us is the tragic fact that they are among 'those who are perishing'. Our relatives and friends are **perishing** in the sense that they are, unless the Lord intervenes, bound for Hell. The word hell is used all too commonly these days in everyday conversation, but all too rarely in the pulpit! John Blanchard refers to this, saying, 'It is never true to say that something "hurts like hell". Nothing hurts like hell!' One shudders to think of it. We must turn on the sunshine of the Good News of the glory of Christ, so that our friends can have the opportunity to receive Him.

When you deal with non-Christians who are **blind** and **dead**, it is all too easy to think of *them* as the enemy and not the victims. The unbeliever is not our enemy. He or she is the **victim** of the enemy!

2 Timothy 2:25-26 gives direction for our prayers We *can* have a part in changing their eternal destination. May God help us to be faithful, for our friends' sake.

6

Listen with Love

Plutarch, the Greek philosopher, who lived just after Christ, said, 'Know how to listen and you will profit even from those who talk badly. Listening is very important Sometimes I have been known to hear, but not to listen to my wife! When we are children, we learn selective listening: we listen to what we want to hear, even though our two small ears may well hear most of what's going around us. If our study encourages us to listen to God more and in turn listen to our loved ones and those friends we are trying to win to Christ, it certainly will change our lives and those of others too!

Listening is vital if we want to know where our friends are coming from spiritually, emotionally, and psychologically. Having listened, we will be in a position to help them. Marriage counsellor, Sue Crookes, has given several points that will help us in such situations. I had the privilege of hearing her at a Covenanter training day some time ago, but I took notes and this is a summary of what she shared.

I. Listen and reflect

Listening attentively is difficult enough. To restrain from speaking after listening, in order to reflect on what has been said, whilst the person continues on another point, is quite an art.

2. Accept

Accept the person just as they are <u>and</u> accept what he or she has to say, or has said, as being how they really feel at that moment.

3. Grasp the whole story

If you are not sure you are getting the whole story, speak up briefly with a, 'Correct me if I'm wrong....' or, 'It seems to me that you are saying....' type of interjection, to clarify your diagnosis of the person's spiritual condition.

4. Empathise and sympathise

Empathy is that emotional effect which impels the listener to actually feel as if the problems and reactions of the person to whom he or she is listening are actually their own. Sympathy is similar: an expression of our fellow feeling and desire to help, but empathy is by far the better of the two!

The best thing that Job's three friends did for

him was that they 'sat on the ground WITH HIM for seven days and seven nights. No-one said a word to him, because they saw how great his suffering was' (Job 2:13). Ezekiel empathised with God's people in their need. 'And there, where they were living, I SAT AMONG THEM for seven days—overwhelmed' (Ezekiel 3:15). When you get close enough to your non-Christian neighbours to share their grief, don't be afraid of silence. Don't fill it with words just because it seems like a long time. God wonderfully speaks in quietness when we get out of the way.

5. Keep it confidential

If anything we are told is confidential, it should not be told to a soul , not even husband or wife! That may cause you grief, but that's better than breaking your word.

6. Scripture and prayer

Scripture and prayer must come into the conversation if we are going to be of any lasting help to our friends.

Dean Rusk once said, 'One of the best ways to persuade others is by listening to them'. All that frantic talking we've done in the past that has got us nowhere! Listening with love is far more effective. Our Lord hasn't just sympathised with us or empathised in our desperate need: '...He too shared in (our) humanity so that by His death He might destroy him who holds the power of death' (the devil!) '...and free those who all their lives were held in slavery by their fear of death' (Hebrews 2:14,15) In that same chapter we're told, 'Because He Himself suffered when He was tempted, He is able to help those who are being tempted'. Hebrews 4:15 tells us, 'For we do not have a high priest who is unable to sympathise with our weaknesses, but we have One who has been tempted in every way, just as we are – yet was without sin'. We as evangelists can know and experience the Lord's 'grace to help us in our time of need'. In turn, we can be like Jesus in listening with love and, at the right moment, share the good news of salvation.

What sort of things will we have to listen to? These days plenty of things will shock us if we have taken an extreme separation position, isolating ourselves from this world. If we are going to be able to help people today we must try to be unshockable...so aware of the devil's devices, that we are not thrown into a panic as the consequences of sin are revealed in the lives of our contacts.

The Holmes-Rahe Stress Scale lists, in order of intensity, the stress rating of events that happen in our lives. Death of a spouse is top of the list with a rating of 100; divorce is next at 73. Getting married scores 50; redundancy 47, and retirement 45. Pregnancy is rated 40; trouble with the boss, 23; etc. Our friends may have very few human agencies to consult as they face these stresses. The Lord wants you to go to your friend in need, listen with love, and eventually lead him or her to Christ. Whether or not people come to place their trust in the Lord is not our responsibility.

We are to find 'common ground' with our unsaved friends and chance contacts, 'so that he will let me tell him about Christ and let Christ save him' (1 Cor. 9:22b, Living Bible).

Will our reaction to the crowds we meet today be, in some small way, that of our blessed Lord? 'When He saw the crowds, He had compassion on them because they were harassed and helpless, like sheep without a shepherd'. Will your friends and neighbours have the benefit of your listening ear today?

7

Talk and Walk

A vital aspect of evangelism is making sure our lives line up with what we say. Jesus said of the Pharisees of His day, 'You must obey them and do everything they tell you. But do not do what they do, for they do not practise what they preach' (Matthew 23:3).

The Pharisees were trying their best to be good, but they failed so often. They had every advantage and were proud of their achievements. Jesus was very hard on them because they knew better, but didn't **talk** and **walk** God's love before the people. Jesus, however, could say to this group, 'Can any of you prove me guilty of sin?' He always lived life perfectly, in total dependence upon and agreement with the Father. Jesus said, 'When you have lifted up the Son of Man, then you will know who I am and that I do nothing on my own, but speak just what the Father has taught Me. The One who sent Me is with Me; He has not left Me alone, for I always do what pleases Him'. Small wonder the thirtieth verse in John chapter 8 says, 'Even as He spoke, many put their faith in Him'. If my life stood up to the example of Jesus, many more would open their hearts to Christ.

In Acts 6:7, it says, 'So the Word of God spread. The number of disciples in Jerusalem increased rapidly, and a **large number of priests** became obedient to the faith'. I wonder how many of the priests to whom Jesus told the truth in no uncertain terms, trusted in Him later?

The talk of Jesus was incredible. No other religious leader has said anything like as profound as the sermons of the Saviour. His talk was from the mouth of God. But His walk as a human being was linked with His words in perfect harmony. He didn't have to say anything to glorify God. When Pilate sent Jesus to Herod, our Lord uttered not a single word. Luke tells us, 'That day Herod and Pilate became friends— before this they had been enemies'.

We place great emphasis today on talk. Politicians and radio preachers talk a lot. Speech is our God-given gift to be able to communicate with one another. But other things have greater influence on the message we leave with someone. Our body language, our appearance, mannerisms, facial expressions and tone of voice are the major ways we make contact with people. If we introduced another category... what people thought of our way of life, perhaps the words would mean even less!

If we don't walk the talk, our Gospel presentation will fall on deaf ears. If we are backslidden in heart, our non-Christian friends may say to themselves, 'What you *are* speaks so loudly, I can't *hear* what you say!' In John's three letters we are urged to 'walk in the light,' to 'walk in obedience', and to 'continue to walk in the truth'.

The way you walk tells other people a great deal about you. If you are injured, it usually shows. When a football team is getting a beating, it shows in the way they walk after yet another goal has been conceded. A young man greeting his girlfriend shows clearly the excitement he is experiencing. On the other hand, a drunk shows the depression his drinking has caused by the way he walks.

Words are our basic building blocks for communicating with other people. Just showing in our lives the presence of Christ only goes so far. The beauties of creation flood our minds with facts about our Creator, but until the good news of what Christ has done is passed on to us, usually through another human being, we never get to see the whole picture of God's plan of salvation.

Colossians 4:5-6 says, 'Be wise in the way you

act towards outsiders; make the most of every opportunity. Let your conversation be always full of grace, **seasoned with salt**, so that you may know how to answer everyone'. What did Jesus mean when he suggested we should be like salt?

I. Salt gives flavour

Jesus, you remember, called His disciples 'the salt of the earth'. Our talk must be similar to the action of salt. It is a seasoning. If our lives and what comes out of our lips make Christ more attractive to our unsaved friends, we are salty.

2. Salt creates thirst

Gracious, relevant, hope-filled words can stimulate further interest in spiritual truth, so we need to be prepared to speak the right word at the right time in the right manner to the right person. Only the Holy Spirit of God can enable us to achieve that, and He loves to arrange the whole thing for us to say words of eternal life.

3. Salt gives freshness

Salt was used as a preservative to prevent meat from spoiling. It kept food from corruption and kept it wholesome. In the same way, salty speech can keep a conversation from degenerating into nothing more than empty, insipid words.

4. Salt lifts up

I was part of a bunch of students from Cheltenham College swimming in the Dead Sea in Israel recently. One young lady was reluctant to believe that it is impossible to sink, even if you can't swim. The water is ten times saltier than normal seas. Once she tried it, she was sure. A lost person is lifted up when our salty speech causes them to think their way towards Christ.

5. Salt can be painful

Physicians in the first century used salt in wounds to keep the infection from spreading. This practice was painful but necessary.

Let's get out of the saltshaker and into the world, and may our salty speech attract others to Christ!

8

Invest in Common Ground

Rebecca Pippert, in her very useful book, *Out of the Saltshaker* says, 'Christians and non-Christians have something in common. We're *both* uptight about evangelism'. Christians are afraid of offending their neighbours. Non-Christians are afraid of being assaulted in their own homes by our occasional forays into their territory.

We decide to have some special evangelistic meetings. Up go the dayglow posters and we prepare to blitz the area! The non-Christians see the signs, run for cover in their foxholes, and hide as best they can until we return to our normal routine of meetings in the church.

In her book *Winsome Witnessing*, Mary Terry writes, 'We must learn that winning to Christ is not talking eloquently or persuasively. It is not arguing convincingly. It is living for Christ every moment of every day. It is loving people. It is sacrificing and denying ourselves and following Jesus. It is bearing a cross. It is agonising over the sins of others. It is toiling in the highways and hedges and compelling them to come in. It is witnessing to what Christ has done for **us.** It is giving a cup of cold water or a bowl of soup in the name of Jesus. It is listening as well as talking, lending a sympathetic ear to a story of failure and woe. It is standing by the sick and suffering, comforting the mourners, helping the man out of work to find a job. It is being honest in every business deal and truthful in every relationship in life. To be a winner of men involves the whole life of a Christian'.

How important is our influence as friends? Win Arn, of the Institute for American Church Growth has put together some percentages to see how people joined the church:

½-1 per cent because of evangelistic crusades or television programmes.

2 per cent came because of special need.

3 per cent just show up on a Sunday and stick.

4 per cent liked the programme the church was offering.

5 per cent were reached by the Sunday School.

6 per cent were influenced by a particular minister.

78 per cent because of the influence of friends and relatives!

All valid types of evangelism mentioned are not to be decried, but personal evangelism seems to be a very fruitful effort. God built a bridge, His name was Jesus. God and man could now be reconnected. At a cost so high we cannot begin to imagine, our Lord Jesus Christ stretched out His arms from Heaven to Earth to provide for the possibility of fellowship with God again.

The bridges we build to our friends are of more value than any human structure because they bring Christ, *the eternal bridge* into the lives of the lost. Those by God's grace who decide to cross will have 'crossed over from death to life,' Jesus said. They have 'eternal life and will not be condemned...' (John 5:24). We must tell our contacts 'there is (only) one God and one mediator between God and men, the man Christ Jesus, Who gave Himself as a ransom for all men...' (1 Timothy 2:5). The previous verse states that 'God our Saviour...wants all men to be saved and to come to a knowledge of the truth'. Our relatives, our colleagues at work, our neighbours, our classmates, our acquaintances, our college chums, all need to hear the good news.

The common ground we share may be the same house or family, the same workplace, school or college. If that's the case, we are already in position to share the good news. They are the obvious points of contact. But what about the school gate, morning and afternoon, when you are collecting the children? What better chance to meet local mums and dads. We can pray for a chance to share in their lives with a view to perhaps sharing Christ later.

If you are fit enough to be involved in a sport, your life will overlap the lives of many who may, later on, after we have extended our friendship bridge, listen to what we have to say about our Saviour. There are many possible common grounds we may use to begin the cultivation process: joining a walking group, boating, swimming. If there isn't a group for your particular interest, start one!

Recently I was invited to be the speaker at what was called, 'Summer Share'. A local Christian and his wife invited their friends to what was described as, 'a totally relaxed summer evening...when we can just enjoy and share each other's company and either sit and chat, or swim, or play badminton, or volleyball if you're truly energetic. When we've become hungry and thirsty, we'll share summer-type refreshments together, and finally Mike Hencher will be sharing some thoughts with us. Time is unimportant; drop in anytime in the evening—you'll be welcome'.

With a bit of imagination we can all find areas

that already overlap the lives of the lost souls around us or, with a little effort on our part, adjust our lives so that there is a group or two of unsaved folk we can get to know and help.

When a soldier was wounded badly in battle and couldn't move, his friend crawled out to get him. He too was hit, but still managed to carry back his mate. When he reached the trench, his friend was dead and he was mortally wounded. His officer was angry. 'It wasn't worth it,' he said. 'But it was, sir,' said the dying man, 'because when I got to him he said, "Jim, I knew you'd come!"'

9

Value the Person

In Luke 15 Jesus told three stories with which all
of us are very familiar. Verse 3 begins, 'Then
Jesus told them this parable: Suppose one of you
has a hundred sheep and loses one of them. Doe
he not leave the ninety-nine in the open country
and go after the lost sheep until he finds it? And
when he finds it, he joyfully puts it on his
shoulders and goes home. Then he calls his
friends and neighbours together and says,
"Rejoice with me; I have found my lost sheep".
I tell you that in the same way there will be more
rejoicing in Heaven over one sinner who repents
than over ninety-nine righteous persons who do
not need to repent.'

Certainly Jesus was teaching, among many
other things, the value of the person—the
individual. We live in a day when many people
feel de-personalised. Have you heard the joke
about the boss who said to an employee, 'Now
then, what makes you feel that we've been
dehumanising you, 624078?' Psychiatrist Dr

Paul Tournier put it well when he said, 'The more we fill our universe with machines, the more important it is that we treat each other as **persons**'. It's not surprising that students march on picket lines with signs like, 'I am a human being: do not bend, fold or mutilate'. We must be very careful not to treat people as numbers – pew fodder or names to file.

Jesus taught and showed in His life how very much He valued the individual person. Jesus had a reputation! He was called the friend of sinners. Should not we, who claim to follow the Lord, have such a reputation? If we do, there will be some who will look down on us and even speak against us. Even people in the church, who haven't got the divine balance on the separation issue, will run us down. But we will know that if the Master loved sinners, we should love them too!

In John 13:15-17, Jesus said, after He had washed the disciples' feet, 'I have set you an example that you should do as I have done for you. I tell you the truth, no servant is greater than his master, nor is a messenger greater than the one who sent him. Now that you know these things, you will be blessed if you do them'. We are to be like our Master, a friend of sinners, remembering all the time that people are people, not projects!

In the 15th chapter of Luke, Jesus is in the thick of things again. '...the Pharisees and the teachers of the law muttered, "This man welcomes sinners, and *eats* with them"'. It is very interesting to read on here, 'Then Jesus told them this parable....' He was teaching many things, but His prime objective was to correct the legalistic, unloving attitudes of the religious leaders. Jesus emphasises the same three points in each of the stories of Luke 15: The Lost Sheep (or The Disciplined Shepherd), the Lost Coin (or The Diligent Woman), and the Lost Son (which really concentrates on the love of The Devoted Father). Let's look at these points as they relate to the first of the parables.

I. Concentrated attention

The Disciplined Shepherd did not say, 'Well, I've got ninety-nine sheep; one more or less, what does it matter; I'm tired and the sheep is probably dead anyway. I won't bother going out tonight to look for it.' No, he valued every one of his sheep, and experienced much personal discomfort until he found it. Winning the world for Jesus Christ begins with <u>one</u>. Trying to win the whole street or neighbourhood to Christ is not a realistic goal. One person, saved, discipled, worshipping and working in the church, is an eternal miracle of great importance.

2. Continued effort

We live in an instant society: instant coffee, instant cash dispensers, instant replays of disputed tennis line calls, instant power at the touch of a switch. Because of this we often expect instant miracles of conversion, without the continued effort of the cultivation of the souls of our friends. The tough job that tests your mettle and spirit is like the grain of sand that gives an oyster a stomach-ache, but after a time it may become a pearl

3. Collective joy

The shepherd's friends rejoiced with him. The woman's neighbours were full of joy too. The father and his family and servants with the exception of the older son, celebrated in style! There's an oriental proverb that says, 'One joy dispels a hundred cares'. Just imagine what would happen in your family, church, or neighbourhood if just one person actually received by faith the grace of God's blessing in his life. Stepping 'from darkness to light, and from the power of Satan to God' (Acts 26:18).

When you value people so much that you spend time with them over an extended period, you share at a very deep level , and have the opportunity to pass on the facts about Christ. There is a bond between you that the Holy Spirit creates. In this loving atmosphere, we usually are able to answer most of their queries and fears about the Christian life, before they trust Christ themselves. Who should disciple them in the early days of their decision to follow Christ? You! Coming to church will be a new and possibly traumatic time; but who will be with them? You!

The result? They become life-long followers of Christ, leading others to the Lord in their turn. All because we concentrated our attention on our needy friends; continued the effort until we were able to share the Gospel, naturally with them; and, in the case of those who trust Christ, enjoying the collective joy of welcoming a new believer into the Family.

10

Answer their Questions

This is where many of us come unstuck: we can't answer our friends' questions! One of the ways we get out of it is to waffle, either changing the question or skating around its edges. Another way out is to panic and relapse into 'expertitis'; in other words, we send our friends to someone we think is an expert, and then we run!

If you are asked a question for which you have no answer, don't waffle. Say something like, 'I really don't know the answer to that, but I will do my best to find one for you.' We don't convince anybody by being the 'answer-man' for any question we try to sort out.

Answering their questions won't save them, but it will bring them to a point where they are able to hear the good news of Christ's salvation with open minds. Those who trust Christ after their questions have been answered, grow so much faster than those who trust the Lord and have to struggle through the problems alone in the early years of walking the Christian pathway.

Twelve tough questions non-Christians will ask

1) How can you be sure there really is a God?

2) If God is good, why do evil and suffering exist?

3) What basis is there for believing in miracles?

4) The Bible is full of errors and myths; how can you believe it?

5) Isn't Christianity just a psychological crutch for weak people?

6) Isn't it narrow-minded to claim that Christ is the only way to God?

7) Will those who have never heard about Christ be condemned?

8) How can Christianity be true when church people are so phoney?

9) Would God reject people who have lived basically good lives?

10) Isn't just believing in Christ for salvation too easy?

11) How much faith do you need to have?

12) Can anyone be sure they will go to Heaven?

Let's answer the first question as if we were explaining it to our friend. This, of course, is just a monologue—the real thing would be a two-way conversation.

The word 'God' can mean different things to different people. Jesus claimed to be the one and only true God, the Creator of the Universe, the One who holds the Universe together right now. Christians believe that the best evidence they have is a personal encounter with Christ which has produced a new way of life for them altogether, described by the Bible as conversion, salvation, or the New Birth. But people who have not yet experienced God for themselves naturally ask for proof. Atheists, who deny the existence of God, usually do so because they believe—notice the word 'believe' (by faith) – that there is no God, because they believe that science disproves God.

Some army officers were discussing religion. One said, 'I was raised on the scientific method; no one has ever been able to prove to me scientifically that God exists'. A Chaplain joined them and said, 'Your problem is similar to one of my own I was raised on the theological method, and no one has ever proved to me theologically that an atom exists'. 'Whoever heard of finding an atom by theology?' the sceptic protested. 'Exactly,' agreed the Chaplain.

If you are asking for proof, use the correct method for each thing you want to prove. Faith in God is based on evidence as surely as science is; the difference is in the kind of evidence on which each is based. If we went to a florist and I picked up a single red rose and said, 'The rose is red', there would be scientific evidence for that statement. But if I had stated, 'The rose is beautiful', I would need other evidence. Science can prove your mother is female, but it can't prove she loves you by producing a test-tube filled with mother's love! To prove God scientifically, you would have to repeat creation and discover a law. That's what science does. It starts with a possibility (an hypothesis) and through repeated experiments comes up with a law. Belief in God is an act of faith.

A very well known playwright was an outspoken atheist for much of his life. In later life he said, 'The science to which I pinned my faith is bankrupt. Its counsels, which should have established the millennium, have led indirectly to suicide. I believed them once and in their name I helped to destroy the faith of millions of worshippers in the temples of a thousand creeds, and now they look at me and they witness the great tragedy of **an atheist who has lost his faith**'. Agnostics are far more common today. They do not say, 'There is no God'; instead they say, 'We do not know whether or not God exists'.

Look at the evidence we do have for God. The Law of Cause and Effect. The evidence of design, throughout the Universe. That to believe this amazing Universe just came together by blind chance, is a statistical impossibility. That all over the globe ancient people believe in one God who made the world, poses the question, are they recalling a far-off day when God was known personally, as the Bible in its first few chapters states?

If we went through this evidence, and much more, you would still be faced with a choice: to have faith in God, based on the evidence, or not. Scientific evidence deals with when and how; the Bible answers the questions, who and why. It says that God made Himself known by many means through the centuries and has actually stepped into time and shown Himself in Jesus Christ.

'If God became man, what would He be like?' His birth would be unique—so was Christ's. He would perform miracles—so did Christ. He would be sinlessly perfect—so was Christ. He would make a universal and long-lasting impression – so did Christ! He would overcome death, being eternal – so did Christ. He would satisfy the spiritual hunger of those seeking salvation – so did Christ. Do you want to prove there is a God? Then study the life, death and resurrection of Christ and respond to His words, 'He who has seen Me', said Jesus, 'has seen (God) the Father'.

Thomas, one of Jesus' disciples, was absent

when Jesus showed Himself alive after His resurrection. Thomas said, 'Unless I see the nail marks in His hands and put my finger where the nails were, and put my hand into His side, I will not believe'. Jesus came again and offered the evidence to Thomas who exclaimed, 'My Lord and my God!'

11

Tell the Truth

There must come a time in the process of evangelism when we state the truth of the Gospel to our friends. *How* to do so is the problem.

Our methodology in this little book is to discover what the Bible says about the subjects we tackle. We cannot look into every reference to evangelism in the Bible, but we can look briefly at two verses from 1 Peter 3 in which we see **seven attitudes** that ideally make up the character of a witness for Christ.

I. Be reverent

'But in your hearts set apart Christ as Lord'. There is a huge difference between receiving Christ as Saviour and making Him Lord of our lives. In ideal circumstances, where the good news of Christ's salvation has been shared correctly, the new convert receives Christ as Saviour and immediately begins to serve Him as Lord. Not in everything to begin with, and, as those of us

who trusted Christ many years ago know only too well, never perfectly. The teaching that sinless perfection is possible in our lives, causes great harm.

Our sincere aim is to let the Lord 'Take my life and let it be consecrated, Lord, to Thee...' to use the opening words of Frances Ridley Havergal's old hymn. But so often, just after we lay our life on the altar, it slips off again because of our sin. Perhaps we still have a problem in living day by day with Christ as our Lord. Don't look for a quick solution; there isn't one! Don't believe that if you have this experience or that blessing, immediately every day of your life will be lived 100 per cent for God. Only one Person ever did that, the Lord Jesus.

It is a daily decision on our part to reverently surrender our lives to the Lord Jesus for Him to use us, or *not* use us, just as He wills. With Christ as Lord, our attempts to tell the truth will be effective.

2. Be ready

'*Always be prepared*...In the previous chapter we spoke of the twelve basic questions people ask about the Christian faith. It is up to us to study the Scriptures thoroughly. Read very widely, not just Christian books, but the works of those men and women who have influenced the lives of the world. This will strengthen our faith enormously and make sure we are ready to give an answer when it is needed.

3. Be reasonable

'...*give an answer to everyone who asks you*....' This is where our faith-stories will have such an impact if they are reasonable. Saying, 'I let Jesus into my heart and He redeemed me from judgement and condemnation', may mean a great deal to you, but your neighbour may not understand more than a few words. Be reasonable; explain what happened to you, putting yourself in his place. Remember, he is blind, dead, and a victim of the enemy! We should remove all barriers to communication from our side.

4. Be real

'...*to give the reason for the hope that you have*...' When we tell the truth, it must be real to us. Have you heard people telling their stories and somehow they don't quite have the ring of truth? People talk of their sinful past so much you begin to wonder if they regret trusting the Lord! I think they feel they must tell a dramatic story. But most of our lives are quite ordinary; that's reality! If we tell the truth of what Jesus has done and is doing in our lives, glorifying Him, our neighbours will listen.

5. Be relaxed

'But do this with gentleness...' In the book 'Mysticism in the East', the story is told of a meeting being addressed by an official stating that science had done away with religion. At the end of his speech he asked the 7,000 listeners for any questions. An old priest asked for time to speak in defence of Christianity. The official agreed but said, 'I can't give you any more than two minutes'. 'I don't need that long', said the priest. He walked slowly down the aisle and stood in front of the huge audience. Smiling, he said, 'Christ is risen!' and, as one man, they shouted back, 'He is risen indeed!' A real pressure situation, but relaxed gentleness won the day. If we argue aggressively, we may well win the argument but we will almost certainly lose the soul.

6. Be respectful

'...and respect....' Many people have lost all respect for themselves. Low self-image, redundancy, divorce, disability, have driven our friends behind their closed doors. Who will go to the elderly, the disabled, the guilty, the lonely, the demoralised? Spend time with them,

showing respect and love, and sooner or later you will be able to share the gospel.

7. Be reapers

Have you ever shared the gospel, or your experience of the Lord, and then said to your friend, 'Would you like to receive Christ?' Too direct for you? How about, 'Is there any reason why you shouldn't trust Christ?' Still a bit foreign to you? Our next study will deal more fully with the subject of being reapers.

12

Expect God's Harvest

The illustration of the cultivation process has made us aware that evangelising is not an immediate thing; it takes time...sometimes a long time. But we must expect God to produce the harvest. 'I planted the seed,' said the Apostle Paul, 'Apollos watered it, *but God made it grow*' (1 Cor. 3:6).

If you are a preacher you will have experienced the dilemma that reaches its height as you close your message: do you make a public appeal or not? Should you invite folk to speak to you afterwards, or do you just say, 'We will now sing our closing hymn, number whatever...'. So-called 'full-time evangelists' can't agree on this, so don't be surprised if you find it difficult. Some preachers do not believe in a get-up-out-of-your-seats-type appeal. Others use the public method very often. God in His grace blesses both approaches.

But if we share the Gospel in a way that does not ask for a verdict, we are not being

faithful. John Ruskin described preaching as '...thirty minutes in which to raise the dead'. If we *really* believe our friends are dead, blind and enslaved as victims of the evil one, we will ask them if they wish to be made alive in Christ, and we should expect a harvest that God has caused to grow. Not everyone we contact will trust Christ, that's obvious; but so often we don't expect anything to happen, and thus go about our witnessing with a sort of resigned reluctance, not expecting anyone to be saved.

Three components of the harvest

a)   The Call
He sent His disciples, 'two by two ahead of Him to every town and place where He was about to go'. The call is for us to go, preferably with another Christian. The wisdom of this becomes clearer the more situations you get into. Alone, there are temptations to face. Alone, the other neighbours may assume the worst. Alone, we may well get discouraged. The wisdom the Lord gave to Solomon is appropriate here, 'Two are better than one because they have a good return for their work: if one falls down, his friend can help him up... Though one may be overpowered, two can defend themselves. A cord of three strands is not quickly broken'. (Ecclesiastes 4:9,10,12). Solomon is saying that

if two are better than one, then three are even better; if we think of the third person as the Lord Himself, three will never be a crowd!

b)   The Crop

Those unique, complex, eternal , human friends of ours are ripe for the harvest. 'The Lord said to His disciples...open your eyes and look at the fields! They are ripe for harvest'. The Lord wants us involved in reaping when the time is right. We do not leave it to our friends to work out for themselves. Some human babies are born without help, but it's best to have a midwife to assist. We can assist our friends to be born again, not inducing a premature birth, but naturally as the Holy Spirit gives conviction of sin, repentance, and faith, and the desire to trust Christ as Saviour.

c)   The Cutters

Labourers swinging scythes have given way to the cutting blades of the combine harvester, but we have not reached the stage where the combine drives itself. Evangelism always has been labour intensive. No better method has been developed over the centuries than one Christian telling one unsaved friend how he too can know the joy of full salvation in Christ Jesus.

Use the printed page, local radio, films,

tapes, telephones, videos, and all the other aids available to us today; but don't forget that, without all these benefits, the early church grew at an amazing rate, largely due to the Christians witnessing where they were. Acts 5:42 says, 'Day after day, in the temple courts and from house to house, they <u>never stopped</u> teaching and proclaiming the good news that Jesus is the Christ'.

Four practical steps in order to reap

a)   **R**: Review the Gospel

A good birth involves a healthy pregnancy. Stranger-to-stranger evangelism often leaves bad experiences in the minds of people who have been pushed too hard, too soon. Friend-to-friend sharing that sometimes has spanned months, even years, is much less open to abuse. Going over the facts of the Gospel with our friend clarifies the decision he is about to make.

b)   **E**: Examine their Objections

If we can remove any remaining objections, we can move on to the birth of a new believer.

c)   **A**: Ask for the Decision

'Are you ready to trust Christ right now?' This question, gently put, will bring out a reply that will tell you what to do next. 'Would you like me to help you pray to receive Christ, or would you prefer to make your commitment alone?' Be

sensitive. The enemy is very active at this point
to hang on to his sinner slave!

d) **P:** Proceed to Discipleship

The next great challenge we face with our
friends.

Discipleship

The process of discipleship, to use our illustration
again, is bringing the grain into the barn and baking
the bread! Our harvest, the human beings we
know and love, is made up of individuals for
whom Christ died. The approach we use, the
methods adopted, and certainly the type of
discipleship we employ, will have to be tailor-
made for the type of person we are trying to
help.

Discipling others is the process by which a
Christian with a life worth emulating commits
himself for an extended period of time to a few
individuals who have been won to Christ, the
purpose being to aid and guide their growth to
maturity and equip them to reproduce themselves
in a third spiritual generation.

Everybody's thrilled when someone is saved,
but that's just the beginning of a new life in Christ.
The hard work of helping that person to
grow up to maturity in Christ is more than just
giving him a Bible and telling him that the Holy

Spirit will lead him. All too often spiritual babies are left to fend for themselves with the minimum of assistance from other Christians.

I. Discipleship is a planned course

'Christian discipleship is a process....' Plan how to help new believers and go to them with the word of encouragement, loving discipline, and general care that will get them out of their spiritual nappies' and into the full armour of God. These new believers are the church leaders of the future. They may take a lot of discipling, but it will be worth it. The cost involved in discipleship is high, but it will renew you as you go back to basics with a young Christian.

A man wounded an elephant in Africa, only to see another one rush to the rescue of its fallen companion. The hunter left the scene, intending to return later for the valuable tusks. He came back after a month and found the animal still alive, in the same spot, unable to move because of its injury. Its mate had cared for it, bringing food and drink regularly. When a member of a herd becomes ill, all the others will stop until the sick one is well again. What a wonderful example of discipleship from the animal kingdom! The Christian church has been called the only army that kills its own wounded!

Paul wrote to the Galatian church (6:1,2) 'Brothers, if someone is caught in a sin, you who are spiritual should restore him gently. But watch yourself, or you also may be tempted. Carry each other's burdens and in this way you will fulfill the law of Christ'.

2. By models of good character

'...*by which a Christian with a life worth emulating*....' To begin with at least, our friends are going to follow our lead. If we are Apostle Pauls we can say, 'Therefore I urge you to imitate me' 1 Cor. 4:16.

But just in case someone gets this out of balance, Paul also said in Ephesians 5:1, 'Be imitators of God'. That's the goal of discipleship, but before the believer comes to maturity he may well copy us! That's a spur to our spirituality, isn't it?

3. As a serious commitment

'...*commits himself*....' This is not an easy-come, easy-go situation; it is a vital link in the process of evangelism that could mean the difference between a life spent for the service of Christ and a Christian life, frail and failing, never shaking off the shackles of the old sin nature. Today's society doesn't like being committed too much. People switch convictions easily. Christians must resist the spirit of the age, to look after number one, first and foremost. Paul points us to Christ, our perfect example, in Romans 15:1-3, 'We who are strong ought to bear with the failings of the weak and not to please ourselves. Each of us should please his neighbour for his good, to build him up. For even Christ did not please Himself....'

4. Under long contract

'...*for an extended period of time...*' Nobody becomes a great sportsperson; a world-famous musician; a scientist who makes a great discovery; a successful homemaker or factory worker, without dedication to the long term. Jesus warned us, before we became His followers, to count the cost. Salvation is God's free gift of His grace, but it cost Him everything He had. Becoming a Christian costs nothing; but being the Christian we are costs everything. Jesus said, '. . .any of you who does not give up everything he has cannot be My disciple'. Remember, just as we seek to serve our brothers and sisters living for Christ, the Holy Spirit lives within us, giving us the power to live out the long contract.

13

Spiritual Battle Training

One day I was talking with a lad about a book which he thought was brilliant. I was a little concerned as the title was 'Mercenary', written by Mike Hoare. It was about his life as a soldier of fortune in what used to be called the Belgian Congo. I was saddened that this lad could be so wrapped up in warfare in his early teens. To be able to make any sensible comment, I asked if I could look through it. What struck me was the sort-of ten commandments for mercenary soldiers that were listed somewhere at the beginning of the book. We'll use these so-called **Commando Rules of Battle** to see how they compare to the rules of engagement for the good soldier of Jesus Christ.

1. Pray to God daily

Surprised? It has been said that there are very few atheists on the battlefield. Sometimes, in the blood, sweat, and tears of battle, men turn to

God. Some men only briefly, but for others it can be a real conversion. Many men found Christ before, during, or after the Falkland conflict.

We all remember the dreadful loss of life in the Heysel Stadium in Belgium. Some Liverpool supporters who were sent back to face trial were very bored so they decided to attend the service run by Prison Chaplain, Theo Kunst. The songbook he uses is one that Billy Graham produced for his Heysel Stadium Crusade back in 1975. One prisoner noted the picture of the stadium on the book cover. The Chaplain explained how Dr Graham had rented the stadium to tell people of Christ and that many had been given new life where recently there was so much death. At the close of the service there was a challenge to trust Christ. One young man received Christ, and there has been a change in his life that has caused amazement among the prison officers.

If mercenaries pray daily, surely we can pray about the battle we are in for the souls of men.

2. Make a fetish of personal cleanliness

'Take pride in your appearance, even in the midst of battle, shave every day without fail.' For those of us who really want to be used by God in any way, there must be daily spiritual cleaning The shaving off,

if you like, of the shadow of sin that so often sticks to us in our society. 'Christ loved the Church and gave Himself up for her to make her holy, cleansing her by the washing with water through the Word....' Ephesians 5:25. If paid warriors can keep themselves clean, we warriors of the Lord need daily washings in the Word.

3. Clean and protect your weapon always

Ephesians 6 tells us of the 'whole armour of God' that we are to put on. Most of the seven items mentioned are defensive, but the last two are weapons for attack. 'The sword of the Spirit' and prayer 'in the Spirit' are offensive weapons to be cleaned and protected. If not, we are like some poor soldiers in the last war, sent into battle with wooden rifles because of shortages of supplies. Our supplies are never in doubt. Our God has promised to 'meet all your needs according to His glorious riches in Christ Jesus' (Phil 4:19).

4. Soldiers in pairs: Be faithful to your mate; loyal to your leaders

Remember Ecclesiastes 4:9? 'Two are better than one...if one falls down, his friend can help him up'. The army of the Lord should be a caring body, faithful to the fellowship, following the leaders.

5. Tell no lies in battle

All information must be accurate or the unit will suffer. I have read prayer letters and statistics from many crusades; too often we read figures that we want to believe but, if we are honest, we can't quite swallow. We never seem to come across these thousands of new believers. Exaggerating the figures won't help our church. We need to know the real numbers attending, an accurate assessment of our impact in the area.

6. Be ready to move at a moment's notice

'Mark all your equipment. Keep it handy at all times. At night develop a routine for finding it.' How many Christians have lost their Bibles? If you've found them, they're often not marked! Moving, or change, has caused many churches to creak. A soldier has to be ready.

7. Look after your vehicle. Do not overload it unnecessarily

These wonderful bodies God has given us are our vehicles, our means of travelling to our neighbours. It goes without saying that we should look after them. But the Devil will either try to make us weak and flabby, so that we don't feel like evangelising, or overload us with work and crush us.

8. Take no unnecessary risks

The wise evangelist will avoid situations that would be a risk to him. The excellent general rule that males deal with males and females with females is thought of as foolish today. The disasters that follow the taking of unnecessary risks are so common we should all carefully think through our plans.

9. Stand-to dawn to dusk; at night have confidence in the sentries

We cannot do everything, in other words. We must learn to delegate. There is no reason for getting annoyed if we do all the cultivation work on our friends and someone else pops up and leads them to Christ.

10. Be aggressive in action, chivalrous in victory, stubborn in defence

US Army General Patton said on one occasion, 'A sound decision violently executed is better than a good plan next week!' Perhaps it will take a sudden action on our part to get us back into the war of evangelism!